Open H

Merriment

MW01114738

LEISURE ARTS, INC. • Maumelle, Arkansas

EDITORIAL STAFF

Vice President of Product Development and
    Publications: Pam Stebbins
Production Director: Tona Jolly
Art Director: Marcus Boyce
Technical Editor: Mary Sullivan Hutcheson
Associate Technical Editors:
    Frances Huddleston and Lois J. Long
Editorial Writer: Susan Frantz Wiles
Senior Graphic Artist: Lora Puls
Graphic Artist: Cailen Cochran
Photography Technical Manager:
    Stephanie Johnson
Prepress Technician: Janie Marie Wright
Contributing Photographers: Mark Mathews
    and Ken West

BUSINESS STAFF

President and Chief Executive Officer:
    Fred F. Pruss
Senior Vice President of Operations:
    Jim Dittrich
Vice President of Retail Sales: Martha Adams
Chief Financial Officer: Tiffany P. Childers
Controller: Teresa Eby
Information Technology Director: Brian Roden
Director of E-Commerce: Mark Hawkins
Manager of E-Commerce: Robert Young

Library of Congress Control Number: 2016946356
ISBN-13/EAN: 978-1-4647-5655-9
UPC: 0-28906-06872-6

Table of Contents

*S*ample all that is *W*onderful

Drop by the Werles' house

Sunday, December 18th
2:00pm

We'll gather to taste
appetizers and desserts

Oh-So
delish!

Open your home to friends and family with a
sampling party of appetizers and miniature
desserts. Savory bites and creamy sweets
bring delicious taste to a fun gathering that
will make a big impression.

OLIVE-WALNUT CROSTINI

- ◆ ½ pound pitted Kalamata and green olives
- ◆ 2 cloves garlic
- ◆ 2 tablespoons capers
- ◆ 1 anchovy packed in olive oil
- ◆ 4 tablespoons olive oil
- ◆ 2 tablespoons balsamic vinegar
- ◆ 1 tablespoon chopped fresh basil
- ◆ ¼ teaspoon black pepper
- ◆ ¼ cup toasted chopped walnut
- ◆ 1 loaf French bread
- ◆ Olive oil
- ◆ Kalamata and green olive slices to garnish

Combine olives, garlic, capers, and anchovy in food processor. Pulse process until olives are coarsely chopped. Add olive oil, vinegar, basil, and pepper; process until well blended. Add walnuts; process until spreading consistency.

Slice bread into ¼" slices. Place on a baking sheet; brush both sides with olive oil. Bake until edges are golden brown in a preheated 350° oven for 15 minutes turning over halfway during baking. Spread olive mixture on bread slices; garnish with olive slices. Serve immediately.

Yield: about 3 dozen servings

CAPRESE BITES

Filling and tomatoes may be prepared ahead then assembled before serving.

- 1 package (8 ounces) fresh mozzarella cheese, cut into 1/2" cubes or smaller depending on size of tomatoes
- 2 tablespoons extra virgin olive oil
- 2 tablespoons white balsamic vinegar
- 1 tablespoon finely chopped fresh basil leaves
- 1/2 teaspoon salt
- 1/2 teaspoon coarse ground pepper
- 16 cherry tomatoes
- 16 small basil leaves
- Salt for tomatoes

Combine cheese cubes, olive oil, vinegar, chopped basil leaves, salt, and pepper in a medium bowl; toss to coat. Cover and chill at least 1 hour.

Cut off top of each tomato. Scoop out pulp and seeds. Salt inside of each tomato. Invert tomatoes onto paper towels; drain 15 minutes. Store tomatoes inverted in an airtight container in refrigerator until ready to stuff.

Place a basil leaf into each tomato. Spoon mozzarella mixture into each tomato onto basil leaf.

Yield: 16 servings

PICADILLO CUPS

To save time on party day, make filling the day before and heat just before serving.

- 1 pound ground chuck
- 1 medium onion, finely chopped
- 1 sweet red pepper, finely chopped
- 3 cloves garlic, minced
- 1/3 cup mango chutney
- 1/4 cup tomato paste
- 1/2 cup dry red wine
- 1 teaspoon ground cinnamon
- 1 teaspoon ground cumin
- 1/2 teaspoon ground oregano
- 1/2 teaspoon salt
- 1/2 teaspoon ground black pepper
- 3 tablespoons capers, drained
- 1/2 bunch cilantro, coarse stems trimmed, chopped
- 1 package (10 ounces) bowl-shaped tortilla chips
- Cilantro leaves to garnish

Brown ground chuck in a large skillet over medium-high heat; remove meat and drain. Reduce heat to medium. Add onion, red pepper, and garlic to skillet; cook just until onion is translucent, stirring frequently. Reduce heat to medium-low. Stir in chutney, tomato paste, red wine, cinnamon, cumin, oregano, salt, and pepper until well blended. Stir in capers; simmer 15 minutes, stirring occasionally, until heated through, and no liquid remains. Stir in chopped cilantro; remove from heat. Spoon a rounded teaspoonful into each chip. Garnish with a cilantro leaf; serve immediately.

Yield: about 96 servings

HAM & BRIE MINI BREAD BITES

- 2 packages (11 ounces each) refrigerated French bread loaf dough
- 1/2 pound shaved deli ham slices, finely chopped (about 2 cups)
- 3 tablespoons apricot preserves
- 1 1/2 tablespoons Dijon mustard
- 1 round (8 ounces) Brie Cheese, rind removed and cheese cut into 1/2" cubes

Cut bread loaf dough into 1/2" slices. Roll each slice into a 1" ball; place 2 inches apart on a greased baking sheet. Bake in a preheated 350° oven for 13 to 15 minutes or until lightly browned. Cool on a wire rack.

Combine chopped ham, apricot preserves, and Dijon mustard in a medium bowl. Cut top from each bread ball; pull dough out of center of ball and press inside smooth to create a hollow area for filling. Place a rounded teaspoon of ham mixture into each ball. Press a cube of cheese into bread ball. Place on a baking sheet; bake in a preheated 350° oven for 5 minutes or until cheese melts. Serve warm.

Yield: about 42 servings

INVITATION

Hand-deliver an invitation to your Sampling Party. Just print the party details on scrapbook paper and layer onto a ribbon-topped cardstock tag. Enclose the invitation in a stamped and colored library book-style envelope. Jumbo rickrack and a pearl brad add an extra layer of festivity to the invite.

CRAB CAKE SLIDERS

Chipotle Spread
- 1 cup Greek-style plain yogurt
- 1 chopped chipotle pepper in adobo sauce (or to taste)
- 1 teaspoon adobo sauce
- 1/2 teaspoon ground black pepper

Crab Cakes
- 3 cans (6 ounces each) crabmeat, drained
- 1/2 cup finely crushed buttery round crackers
- 1/2 cup finely chopped green pepper
- 1/2 cup finely chopped sweet red pepper
- 3 tablespoons minced onion

- 2 teaspoons minced fresh parsley
- 1/3 cup mayonnaise
- 1 large egg, beaten
- 1 teaspoon Worcestershire sauce
- 1 teaspoon dry mustard
- 1/2 lemon, juiced
- 1/4 teaspoon garlic powder
- 1/4 teaspoon salt
- 1/4 teaspoon ground black pepper
- pinch of cayenne pepper
- Flour for coating
- Extra virgin olive oil for frying
- Small rolls, lettuce leaves, and tomato slices for serving

For spread, combine all ingredients and chill for 1 hour.

For crab cakes, combine all ingredients except crabmeat, flour, and olive oil in a large bowl. Gently mix in crabmeat. Form into 2" diameter cakes and chill for 1 hour. Coat both side of cakes with flour. Cook crab cakes in hot olive oil (depth of 1/2") about 4 minutes each side or until lightly browned.

To assemble sandwiches, cut the rolls in half and spread with Chipotle Spread. Fill the roll with a crab cake, lettuce, and tomato. Serve warm.

Yield: about 40 sliders

MINI PUMPKIN CHEESECAKES ·······················

Make these individual cheesecakes with a mini cheesecake pan.

Crust

- ¾ cup ginger snap cookie crumbs
- ½ cup finely chopped pecans
- ¼ cup firmly packed brown sugar
- 2 tablespoons butter, melted

Filling

- 1 cup canned pumpkin
- 2 eggs
- 1 teaspoon vanilla extract
- 1 tablespoon flour
- 1 teaspoon pumpkin pie spice
- ¼ teaspoon salt
- 2 packages (8 ounces each) cream cheese, softened
- ½ cup firmly packed brown sugar
- ¼ cup granulated sugar
- Whipped cream to garnish
- Toasted chopped pecans to garnish

For crust, combine cookie crumbs, pecans, and sugar in a medium bowl until well blended; stir in melted butter. Press 1 tablespoon of mixture into each opening of a 12-opening nonstick mini cheesecake pan with removable bottoms. Bake in a preheated 350° oven for 8 minutes.

For filling, beat pumpkin, eggs, vanilla, flour, pumpkin pie spice, and salt in a medium bowl. In a large bowl, beat cream cheese and sugars until fluffy. Add pumpkin mixture to cream cheese mixture; beat until well blended. Spoon 2 tablespoons of filling into each crust-filled opening. Bake for 20-25 minutes or until filling is set. Cool on a wire rack. Run a knife or spatula around edge of each cheesecake. Push each cheesecake up out of pan and remove bottom. Transfer to a serving plate. Cover and refrigerate at least 2 hours or overnight.

To serve, place a teaspoonful of whipped cream on each cheesecake. Garnish with pecans.

Yield: 24 cheesecakes

CREAMY LIME SHOTS

Make filling and topping a day ahead to chill.

Filling

- 4 egg yolks
- 1 can (14 ounces) sweetened condensed milk
- $^1/_3$ cup freshly squeezed lime juice (about 2 limes)

Topping

- $^1/_4$ cup sour cream
- 1$^1/_2$ teaspoons confectioners sugar
- Graham crackers to serve
- Lime zest to garnish

For filling, combine egg yolks, sweetened condensed milk, and lime juice in a medium saucepan over low heat. Cook, stirring constantly, until mixture reaches 160° (about 10 minutes). Remove from heat. Transfer to a bowl; cover with plastic wrap directly on the filling. Cover and chill overnight.

For topping, combine sour cream and confectioners sugar in a small bowl; stir until well blended. Cover and refrigerate overnight.

To serve, crumble graham crackers. Layer graham cracker crumbs and filling in a 2-ounce shot glass. Spoon sour cream topping on top. Garnish with lime zest.

Yield: 9 servings

LEMON SHORTBREAD TARTLETS

Purchased lemon curd and tartlet shells are shortcuts for these desserts!

- $^2/_3$ cup mascarpone cheese, softened
- $^1/_3$ cup heavy cream
- 3 tablespoons confectioners sugar
- 24 shortbread tartlet shells
- 1 jar (10 ounces) lemon curd
- Finely chopped crystallized ginger to garnish

In a medium bowl, beat mascarpone cheese, cream, and confectioners sugar until it begins to hold its shape. Cover and chill until ready to serve.

Place tartlet shells on a serving plate. Place 2 teaspoons of lemon curd in each shell. Spoon 1 teaspoon mascarpone mixture on top. Garnish with crystallized ginger.

Yield: 2 dozen tartlets

AMARETTO PEACH DESSERTS

- ◆ 1 package (16 ounces) frozen peaches, thawed and chopped
- ◆ $^1/_4$ cup orange juice
- ◆ $^1/_2$ cup sugar
- ◆ 1 tablespoon cornstarch
- ◆ $^1/_8$ teaspoon salt
- ◆ 2 tablespoons amaretto
- ◆ Mini almond biscotti
- ◆ 1 quart premium vanilla ice cream, softened

Place peaches and orange juice in a large saucepan over medium-high heat. In a small bowl, combine sugar, cornstarch, and salt; stir into peach mixture. Stirring frequently, bring mixture to a boil; reduce heat to medium low. Cook mixture 10 minutes or until peaches are tender and syrup has thickened. Remove from heat; stir in amaretto. Cool in pan.

To serve, spoon 2 tablespoons of peaches into each mini serving dish. Place a mini biscotti into edge of dish. Top filling with a spoonful of softened ice cream. Serve immediately.

Yield: 10 servings

CHOCOLATE MOUSSE

- ◆ $^3/_4$ cup butter, cut into pieces
- ◆ 1 cup whipping cream, divided
- ◆ 5 eggs, separated
- ◆ 1 package (6 ounces) semisweet chocolate chips
- ◆ $^1/_4$ cup chocolate-flavored liqueur
- ◆ $^2/_3$ cup granulated sugar
- ◆ 2 tablespoons water
- ◆ $^1/_4$ teaspoon cream of tartar
- ◆ $^1/_2$ cup sifted confectioners sugar
- ◆ 1 teaspoon vanilla extract
- ◆ Caramel ice cream topping and coarse sea salt, for garnish

Combine butter, $^1/_4$ cup cream, and egg yolks in top of a double boiler. Whisking constantly, cook over simmering water until mixture reaches 160 degrees (about 10 minutes). Remove from heat and stir in chocolate chips; stir until smooth.

Transfer to a small bowl and cool to room temperature. Stir in liqueur.

Combine egg whites, granulated sugar, water, and cream of tartar in top of double boiler. Whisking constantly, cook over simmering water until mixture reaches 160 degrees (about 9 minutes). Transfer to a large bowl and beat until stiff peaks form. Gently fold chocolate mixture into egg white mixture. Spoon mousse into mini serving dishes, loosely cover, and chill until ready to serve.

Place a medium bowl and beaters from an electric mixer in freezer until well chilled. In chilled bowl, whip remaining $^3/_4$ cup cream until soft peaks form. Add confectioners sugar and vanilla extract; beat until stiff peaks form. Garnish with whipped cream, caramel topping, and a sprinkling of sea salt.

Yield: 8 servings

Christmas
is for kids

Children love to be involved in holiday creativity! Count them in with this simple plan for a tree that is all theirs, with easy ornaments and garlands to craft. Finger-wrapped pom-pom ornaments provide a big splash of color when mixed with craft-stick snowflakes, yarn wreaths, and strings of paper circles and pennants. No-sew felt elf hats enhance the camaraderie. Adults can help fashion additional accents, including cute paper clay elves that make wonderful keepsakes.

Tree

The colorful tree showcases children's handicrafts. Hang wooden "snowflakes," yarn pom-poms and wreaths, and paper garlands on a simple feather tree. Gather fabric around the tree base in anticipation of the gifts from Santa. The kids will enjoy hours of fun making the decorations for their tree.

WOODEN SNOWFLAKES

For each snowflake, arrange 3 craft sticks to look like a snowflake and glue the centers together. Glue a clear nylon thread hanger to the snowflake. Punch small and large circles from colorful scrapbook paper or cardstock. Glue to the front and back of the snowflake tips and center.

POM-POM ORNAMENTS

Make finger poms (page 21) in various sizes using different color yarns. Tie a yarn loop around the middle for a hanger.

YARN WREATHS

Wrap yarn around a small foam wreath, gluing the yarn ends on the wrong side. Trim the wreath with contrasting rick-rack and embroidery floss, again gluing the ends on the wrong side. Tie a small finger pom (page 21) to the wreath.

PAPER GARLANDS

For the circle garland, punch 1" circles from double-sided patterned cardstock. Leaving very long thread tails at the beginning and the end, machine sew the circles together.

For the pennant garland, trace the pattern, page 64, onto tracing paper and cut out. Use the pattern to cut pennants from double-sided patterned cardstock. Leaving very long thread tails at the beginning and the end, machine sew the pennants together.

Paper Clay Elves

- 1.8" (47mm) foam ball for each elf head and 2.8" x 3.8" (72mm x 98mm) foam egg for each elf body
- 10" length of 1/4" diameter dowel for each elf
- 3⅞" diameter x ⅜" papier-mâché disc for each base
- Creative Paperclay®
- Snow-Tex™ textural medium
- mica flakes
- acrylic paints and paintbrushes
- black permanent marker
- 20-gauge wire
- trims such embroidery floss for hair, glittery pom-poms, and felt for buttons
- sandpaper
- craft glue
- wire cutters
- needle-nose pliers
- drill and small bit
- handsaw
- craft knife

1. Cut a small notch in the head so it will rest on the tip of the body and glue them together. Cut two 2"-long arms and two 3"-long legs from the dowel for each elf. Drill a small hole through one end of each dowel arm; set arms aside. Cut holes in the base for the legs and glue them in place. Insert the legs in the bottom of the body.

2. Cover the framework with Paperclay, dipping your finger in water and smoothing the clay as you go. Build the clay up in the cheek, nose, and boot areas. Size and placement of the cheeks and nose can change the expression of the elf. Form mittens at the arm ends.

3. Make separate ear pieces and attach to the head while they are wet. Shape a cap separately and place on the head. The cap can stand upright or tilt to one side. Allow to dry overnight.

Elf Hat

- 27" felt square for hat
- 8" x 27" felt piece for brim
- jumbo rickrack
- felt scraps for circles
- medium weight yarn for pom-pom
- fabric glue

1. Measure around the child's head right above the eyebrows. For heads 21" and less, photocopy the patterns on page 60 at 255%; for heads greater than 21", photocopy the patterns at 277%. Tape the pieces together. Use the patterns to cut a hat from felt and a brim from a contrasting felt color. If desired, cut assorted size felt circles.
2. Glue the brim, circles, and rickrack to the hat.
3. Overlap the hat bottom edge by 2" and pin. Try the hat on the child and adjust as necessary. Glue the overlapped areas together.
4. Make a 2^1/$_2$" pom-pom (page 56) and glue to the hat point.

4. Lightly sand, then paint the figure and each arm. Add facial features with the black marker. Apply Snow-Tex and mica flakes to the base.
5. Attach each arm to the body with a 4" wire length, poking the wire into the body; coil the wire ends to secure.
6. Glue floss hair to the head as desired. Glue a glittery pom-pom to the hat. Add felt buttons if desired.

"Joy" Banner

- three 4" diameter wooden embroidery hoops
- felt scraps for letters
- three 6" squares of fabric
- embroidery floss
- embroidery needle
- jumbo rickrack
- medium weight yarn
- tracing paper

1. Trace the patterns (page 59) onto tracing paper; cut out. Use the patterns to cut the letters from felt. Center a letter on each fabric square and use *Running Stitches* (page 57) to attach the letter to the square. Insert the fabric squares in the hoops; trim the excess fabric.
2. Make 4 finger poms (page 21). Use floss to sew the finger poms and the hoops to the rickrack.

Gift Boxes

- papier-mâché boxes
- acrylic paint and paintbrushes
- fine-grit sandpaper
- matte-finish clear acrylic spray sealer
- yarn

Paint each box as desired, inside and out. After the paint is dry, lightly sand some areas of the box. Working in a well-ventilated area, spray the box with the acrylic sealer. Place the gift in the box and tie with yarn. Embellish with finger poms (page 21) or a yarn wreath (page 15).

Stockings

For each stocking:

◆ two 13" x 24" fabric pieces for stocking (we used a brushed twill)

◆ 9" x 10" fabric piece for heel and toe

◆ fabric scraps for appliqués

◆ ⅝ yard of jumbo rickrack

◆ medium weight yarn for pom-pom

◆ 9" length of twill tape for hanger

◆ embroidery floss

◆ trims, such as buttons and medium rickrack

◆ paper-backed fusible web

◆ embroidery needle

◆ clear nylon thread

When sewing, always match the right sides and raw edges and use a ¹/₂" seam allowance.

1. Photocopy the patterns on pages 62-63 at 150%. Use the stocking pattern to cut 2 stocking pieces from fabric, cutting one in reverse.

2. Fuse the web to the wrong side of the heel/toe and appliqué fabrics. Use the patterns to cut a heel and toe and to cut the desired appliqués.

3. Fuse the heel, toe, and appliqués to the stocking front. Use clear thread to zigzag stitch jumbo rickrack 2¹/₄" below the top edge and along the heel and toe inner edges.

4. Work *Running Stitches* (page 57) on the appliqués and for the reindeer's antlers. Sew buttons and medium rickrack to the designs as desired.

5. Leaving the top edge open, sew the stocking front and back together. Clip the curved seam allowances, turn the stocking right side out, and press. Press ¹/₄" and then 1" to the wrong side along the top edge. Sew close to the first fold with clear thread.

6. Make a 3" finger pom (page 21). Sew the pom and twill tape hanger to the stocking corner.

Photo Globes

- clear acrylic separating ball ornaments
- black and white photos (or copies)
- cardstock
- thin cardboard
- clear nylon thread
- craft glue
- ribbon
- felt scraps, tiny pom-poms, small beads, ribbons, seasonal brads, etc. to embellish the photos

Separate the ornament pieces. Cut the photo about 1/2" smaller than the ornament. Cut a piece of cardstock and cardboard the same size. Embellish the photo as desired. With the cardboard in the middle, sandwich a folded 12" length of clear thread in between the cardstock and photo circles; glue. Allow to dry. Pull the clear thread through the opening at the top of the ornament and pull taut to bring the image close to the top; knot tightly. Knot the thread ends together to form the hanger. Close the ornament and tie a ribbon bow at the top.

Pom-Pom Flowers

- assorted yarns
- 1/4" diameter dowels
- green acrylic paint and a paintbrush
- green felt scraps
- buttons (optional)
- low-temp glue gun

1. Cut the dowels into 9"-12" lengths and paint green.
2. Photocopy the leaf pattern (page 61) at 118%. Use the pattern to cut leaves from felt. Make a finger pom (right) for each flower. Glue a flower and leaves to each dowel; add a button to the center if desired.

Finger Pom

Winding yarn around your fingers is a fast and easy way to make a pom-pom. Here's the step-by-step instructions.

1. Set aside a 12" yarn length. Pulling the yarn directly from the skein and holding the end with your thumb, wrap the yarn around your fingers. Lots of wraps makes a thick, dense finger pom; less wraps makes a looser, more freeform finger pom.
2. Pull the pom-pom off your fingers. Knot the 12" yarn length around the middle of the wrapped area and cut the looped ends. Trim the finger pom to the desired size.

gifts from Nature

Let the timeless beauty of creation transform your home into a serene holiday setting. Peaceful plants thrive in rustic planters and imaginative terrariums. Burlap gift bags get woodsy texture from pinecones and moss. Simple pine sprigs and berries are easy to stitch on stockings or a pillow. Bits of faded papers and metals add timeworn personality.

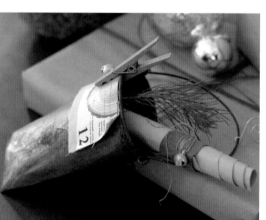

Crewel Pillow

- two 17" x 17" fabric squares (we used linen)
- crewel embroidery wool yarn (red, brown, gold, olive, dark olive, grey)
- crewel embroidery needle
- 16" x 16" pillow form
- 6mm red and dyed pom-poms (page 56)
- fusible tear-away embroidery stabilizer
- tissue paper
- fabric glue

1. Follow the manufacturer's instructions to fuse the stabilizer to the wrong side of one fabric square.
2. Photocopy the pattern, page 59, at 221%. Trace onto tissue paper. Center and pin the tissue paper pattern on the right side of the fabric square with stabilizer on the back. Follow the *Stitching Key* to embroider the design. Carefully tear away the tissue paper and stabilizer.
3. Matching the right sides and raw edges and leaving an opening for turning and stuffing, use a 1/2" seam allowance to sew the pillow squares together. Clip the corners and turn the pillow right side out.
4. Insert the pillow form into the pillow. Slipstitch the opening closed.
5. Glue the pom-poms to the embroidered branches as desired.

Tree Décor

Draping clear lights on the tree showcases its quiet beauty, while placing the tree, stand and all, in a whiskey half-barrel makes for a simple display.

Decorate the tree with garlands that are easy to make. Thread dyed pom-poms (page 56) onto cotton thread for a Berry Garland. Cut thin discs from a 3" tree trunk or branch, drill a small hole at the top, and use wire loops to hang the discs on a jute length to complete the Tree Trunk Disc Garland.

Scatter clusters of pinecones that have been joined together by wrapping thin wire between the scales.

Clear glass 4" diameter ornaments make Tiny Terrariums. Use tweezers to add brown and green moss, lichen, and tree bark to each ornament. Nestle a spider plant "plantlet" or two amongst the moss. Lightly mist the ornament interior and replace the cap and hanger.

Stockings

SIMPLE STOCKING

- two 14" x 24" fabric pieces (we used linen)
- crewel embroidery wool yarn for hanger (we used ivory and light olive)
- $^7/_8$" diameter wood button

When sewing, always match the right sides and raw edges and use a $^1/_2$" seam allowance, unless otherwise instructed.

1. Photocopy the pattern, pages 58-59, at 160%. Use the pattern to cut 2 stockings (1 in reverse) from fabric.
2. Leaving the top edge open, sew the stocking pieces together. Clip the curved seam allowances and turn the stocking right side out; press.
3. Press the top edge $^1/_4$" to the wrong side twice; hem.
4. For the hanger, cut 3 15" yarn lengths and knot the lengths together about 3" from one end. Braid the lengths for 5" and knot again. Trim about 3" from the knot. Fold the length in half and sew to the stocking corner. Use another yarn length to sew the button to the stocking.

CUFFED STOCKING

- two 14" x 24" fabric pieces for stocking and a 13" x 8" fabric piece for cuff (we used linen)
- crewel embroidery wool yarn (ivory, grey)
- crewel embroidery needle
- small faux pinecones
- $^7/_8$" diameter wood button
- fusible tear-away embroidery stabilizer

When sewing, always match the right sides and raw edges and use a $^1/_2$" seam allowance, unless otherwise instructed.

1. Photocopy the pattern, pages 58-59, at 160%. Use the pattern to cut 2 stockings (1 in reverse) from fabric. Follow the manufacturer's instructions to fuse the stabilizer to the wrong side of one stocking heel and toe. Use ivory yarn to *Backstitch* (page 57) the heel and toe areas on the stocking with stabilizer on the back. Carefully tear away the stabilizer.

2. Leaving the top edge open, sew the stocking pieces together. Clip the curved seam allowances and turn the stocking right side out; press.
3. For the cuff, match the long edges and sew the side seams. Turn the cuff right side out and press. Matching the cuff right side to the stocking wrong side and placing the finished sides of the cuff along the heel side seam, sew the cuff to the stocking top. Fold the cuff to the right side and press.
4. Wrap a yarn length between the upper scales of each pinecone; knot the yarn, hiding the knot among the scales. Use the yarn ends to sew the pinecones to the cuff.
5. Follow Step 4 of the Simple Stocking, left, to attach the hanger.

EMBROIDERED STOCKING

- two 14" x 24" fabric pieces (we used linen fabric)
- tissue paper
- crewel embroidery wool yarn (light olive, grey)
- crewel embroidery needle
- jute twine
- thin red jute twine
- 4 pearl brads
- fusible tear-away embroidery stabilizer

When sewing, always match the right sides and raw edges and use a $^1/_2$" seam allowance, unless otherwise instructed.

1. Photocopy the patterns, pages 58-59, at 160%. Use the stocking pattern to cut 2 stockings (1 in reverse) from fabric.
2. Follow the manufacturer's instructions to fuse the stabilizer to the wrong side of 1 stocking under the area for the pine sprig. Trace the pine sprig pattern onto tissue paper. Pin the tissue paper pattern to the right side of the stocking. Follow the *Stitching Key* to embroider the design. Carefully tear away the tissue paper and stabilizer.
3. Use the light olive yarn to *Couch Stitch* (page 57) 2 jute twine lengths to the cuff area of the embroidered stocking piece. For each berry, wrap the red jute twine into a small, loose ball. Flatten the ball and securely tack to the cuff area. Attach a brad through each berry and into the stocking.
4. Follow Steps 2-4 of the Simple Stocking, upper left, to complete the stocking, omitting the button.

Burlap Gift Bags

POUCH

Approx. finished size: 10$\frac{1}{2}$"w x 9$\frac{1}{2}$"h

- 11$\frac{1}{2}$" x 24" piece of burlap
- 3"h chipboard letter
- sheet moss
- dyed pom-poms (page 56)
- craft glue
- thin red jute twine
- $\frac{7}{8}$" diameter wood button

1. Press each short end of the burlap piece $\frac{1}{4}$" to the wrong side twice; hem.
2. Matching the right sides, fold one short end up 9$\frac{1}{2}$". Using a $\frac{1}{2}$" seam allowance, sew the side seams. Turn the pouch right side out.
3. Press the remaining raw edges $\frac{1}{4}$" to the wrong side twice; hem.
4. Glue moss and pom-poms to the chipboard letter. Glue the letter to the pouch.
5. Place a gift in the pouch and wrap the red twine around the pouch. Thread the red twine ends through the button holes and tie in a bow.

BOTTLE BAG

- 7$\frac{1}{2}$" x 29" piece of burlap
- thin red jute twine
- letter brads to spell message
- faux pinecone sprig

1. Matching the right sides and short ends, use a $\frac{1}{2}$" seam allowance to sew the burlap bag sides together. Turn the bag right side out.
2. Pull a few threads from the top edge to create fringe. Work red twine *Straight Stitches* (page 57) in a "V" pattern about $\frac{3}{4}$" below the fringe. With 2 strands of red twine, work loose *Running Stitches* about 2$\frac{1}{2}$" below the fringe; leave very long tails on the Running Stitches. Insert the brads into the burlap, spelling out your holiday message.
3. Place a bottle in the bag and pull the red twine tails tight. Tie a bow, catching the pinecone sprig in the knot.

For presents that come in bottles or book jackets, Burlap Gift Bags will keep them uniquely undercover until December twenty-fifth.

Frame Terrarium

To make a rustic terrarium, gather three 10"x20" frames and two 8"x10" frames, eight 2" 90-degree corner braces, wood screws and screwdriver, silicone adhesive, two 2" hinges, a handle for the lid, and a piece of aluminum flashing and a ¼" thick piece of plywood that fits the outer dimensions of one larger frame. If the frames do not include glass, you'll also need glass for each frame.

Join the two large frames and two small frames into a box shape, placing a corner brace at each corner. For the lid, join the last large frame to the box top with the hinges. Add the handle to the lid.

Adhere the flashing to the box bottom; adhere the plywood to the flashing. Place the glass in each frame and seal in place with adhesive.

Glass Terrarium

◆ covered glass container

◆ pea gravel

◆ horticultural charcoal

◆ fresh potting soil

◆ small plants with similar care requirements

◆ stones

1. Wash the container with hot soapy water and dry thoroughly.
2. Place a 1" layer of pea gravel, a ¹/₂" layer of charcoal, and a 2"-3" layer of soil in the container.
3. Remove the plants from their pots and gently tease out the roots, removing any excess soil from the root ball. Place the plants in the soil, tamping the soil down around each plant.
4. Arrange stones and other decorative elements among the plants. Lightly mist the plants and replace the cover. The covered terrarium should be a self-contained mini ecosystem and not need additional watering. If you make an open top terrarium, the plants will need periodic misting.

Please an indoor gardener by potting up a basket of succulents or fresh herbs to be placed in a sunny window. You'll find these warm-weather plants in many grocery stores year-round.

Gift Baskets

Wood berry baskets, lined with natural-colored shredded paper, are a great way to give small potted herbs or succulents. Pot the plant in a small hypertufa pot (page 39). Place the pot, a votive candle, a pinecone, and an ornament or other small gift in the basket. Write the recipient's name on a metal plant marker. Jute twine, holly leaves, and small bells added to the basket make for a thoughtful presentation.

Holiday Wreath & Banner

WREATH

- 22" x 13" oval grapevine wreath
- linen fabric
- paper-backed fusible web
- thin red jute twine
- permanent fabric marker
- pinecones
- assorted size dyed pom-poms (see page 56)
- tracing paper
- hot glue gun and glue sticks

1. Trace the mini banner pattern (page 58) onto the paper side of the web 5 times, leaving about ½" between each shape. Fuse the web to the wrong side of the linen fabric. Cut out each shape and remove the paper backing. Lay shapes, wrong side up, on the work surface side by side about ¼" apart. Lay a 24" length of red twine through the centers of the shapes; fold the shapes in half and fuse together, fusing the twine in between. Write "m, e, r, r, y" on mini banner pieces.
2. Tie the mini banner to the wreath. Glue the pinecones and dyed pom-poms to the wreath.

BANNER

- burlap
- cardstock (red, dark green, light green, olive)
- grey faux suede fabric
- paper-backed fusible web
- thin green jute twine
- thick twine
- hand sewing needle with large eye
- tracing paper
- craft glue

1. For the burlap pattern, photocopy the pattern (page 64) at 197%. Use the pattern to cut 9 burlap shapes.
2. For the cardstock pattern, photocopy the pattern at 189%. Use the pattern to cut 9 cardstock shapes.
3. Fold the top edge of each burlap shape 1" to the right side. Use green twine to work *Running Stitches* (page 57) near the top to create a casing for the thick twine.
4. Print "christmas" letters (about 2"-2½" high) from your computer; cut out each letter. Fuse the web to the wrong side of the faux suede fabric. Place the printed letters, wrong side down, about ½" apart on the paper backing and draw around each letter. Cut out each letter and remove the paper backing. Fuse the letters to the burlap shapes. Glue the burlap shapes to the cardstock shapes, taking care to not glue the casings closed.
5. Cut the desired length of thick twine and thread it through the burlap casings.

Cards & Tags

Cards and tags can easily be personalized with old family photos, chipboard letters and rub-on letters and numbers. Here's a variety of ideas for making holiday greetings.

- ◆ Look for cards, tags, and envelopes in kraft paper or other handmade papers.
- ◆ Add seasonal color with red, green, and cream scrapbook papers, cardstock, dried holly leaves, thin jute twine, and linen fabric scraps.
- ◆ *Size* (page 56) old photos to fit the card; photocopy the photo. Mat the copies with cardstock and photo corners.
- ◆ Chipboard letters can be painted or wrapped in thin jute twine.
- ◆ Mini bells, small word charms, and decorative brads add a bit of sparkle.
- ◆ Use nature-related images and text from old encyclopedias, dictionaries, magazines, or books.

Reach out to friends this year with handcrafted Cards and Tags.

Countdown Pails

Count down the final days before Christmas with rusty pails that are decorated with nature-themed tags. To make each tag, cut an image from an old book, encyclopedia, dictionary, or magazine that pertains to trees or plants. Add rub-on numbers (we used 1-12). Machine stitch the image to a larger fabric piece; use contrasting thread to hand sew a bell on the tag. Clip the tag to the pail with a clothespin.

Wrap the stair banister with greenery and hang the pails from the garland with swirly ornament hooks. Fill each pail with a special treat or small gift.

Hypertufa Pots

*Hypertufa is similar to concrete, but more lightweight and porous. It can be formed into any size and shape planting pot by using a mold. Anything that has an interesting shape can be used as a mold—a disposable nursery pot, a bin, a bowl, take-out containers, an old basket, paper milk cartons—the possibilities are endless. You'll also need an "inner mold"; smaller nursery pots, milk cartons, and other disposable food containers are perfect (**Photo 1**).*

- ◆ perlite
- ◆ Portland cement
- ◆ peat moss
- ◆ cooking spray

- ◆ large plastic tub or bin
- ◆ rubber gloves
- ◆ dust mask
- ◆ water

- ◆ mold (see above)
- ◆ ¹/₂" diameter wooden dowel
- ◆ plastic bags
- ◆ wire brush or sandpaper

1. Wearing rubber gloves to protect your hands and a dust mask to avoid breathing in cement dust, mix equal parts of perlite, cement, and peat moss in the large tub (**Photo 2**). Add water, a bit at a time, until the mix is of a cottage cheese consistency (**Photo 3**).

2. Generously spray the inside of the mold with cooking spray. Place the hypertufa mix into the mold a handful at a time, pressing the mixture firmly against the mold bottom. Keep adding hypertufa until the bottom is about ³/₄"-1" thick. Make a drainage hole (or holes) in the bottom by pushing the dowel into the bottom (**Photo 4**). Begin to add hypertufa around the mold sides, again firmly pressing it against the mold. Make the sides about ³/₄" thick and have them go up to the mold rim. Press the hypertufa firmly to remove any air pockets.

3. Spray the outside of the inner mold and place in the mixture. Add more hypertufa as necessary to complete the pot. You can smooth the top edge or leave it rough.

4. Cover the pot with a plastic bag (**Photo 5**) and let dry about 48 hours.

5. Remove the plastic bag. Remove the pot from the mold (it will not be completely dry). Rough up the pot exterior with the wire brush or sand paper if desired (**Photo 6**). Let the pot sit (but not in direct sun) for 2-3 weeks to completely dry.

Santa
stop here!

Colorful snacks create an irresistible setting where kids —
and the young at heart — can show their excitement over
Santa's upcoming visit. From Christmas Tree Sandwich
Kabobs to Peanut Butter Cookie Pops and Berry Slush,
these treats offer yummy holiday flavor. Kid-friendly finger
foods and dips make the party complete!

CHRISTMAS TREE SANDWICH KABOBS

Have ingredients ready to make kabobs shortly before serving.

- ◆ **2 whole wheat mini bagels, sliced and halved**
- ◆ **8 small dill pickles**
- ◆ **8 slices thinly sliced ham, rolled and trimmed**
- ◆ **4 slices thinly sliced cheese, cut in half and rolled**
- ◆ **8 fresh pineapple chunks**
- ◆ **8 cherry tomatoes**
- ◆ **8 wooden skewers**
- ◆ **Leaf lettuce**

Thread bagel pieces, lettuce, pickles, rolled ham slices, and rolled cheese slices onto wooden skewers. Trim pineapple chunks into a flat top triangle and add to skewer. Top with a tomato. Cover with plastic wrap and chill until ready to eat.
Yield: 8 kabobs

CHEESY CHICKEN TIDBITS

Suit your family's taste buds by adding additional seasoning to spice up these favorites.

- ◆ 1 cup all-purpose flour
- ◆ 1 teaspoon salt
- ◆ 1 teaspoon ground pepper
- ◆ 2 eggs, beaten
- ◆ ½ cup milk
- ◆ 2 cups crushed cornflakes
- ◆ 1 cup finely shredded Cheddar cheese
- ◆ 2 pounds fresh chicken breast tenderloins, cut into pieces

In a small bowl, combine flour, salt, and pepper. In another small bowl, combine eggs and milk. In a third small bowl, combine cornflake crumbs and cheese. Dip chicken pieces in flour, egg mixture, and then into cornflake crumb mixture, making sure that pieces are coated on both sides. Place chicken on a greased baking sheet. Bake in a preheated 375° oven for 20 to 25 minutes or until golden brown. Serve warm.
Yield: about 30 tidbits

BERRY SLUSH

Using frozen banana chunks instead of ice keeps this drink from getting watered down.

- ◆ 1 banana, peeled, cut into chunks, and frozen
- ◆ 1 cup frozen whole strawberries
- ◆ 1 cup frozen blueberries
- ◆ 1 cup strawberry yogurt
- ◆ 1 to 2 cups berry juice blend

In a blender, combine all ingredients; blend until smooth, adding additional juice for preferred consistency.
Yield: about 4 cups

KID-FRIENDLY DIPPING SAUCE

Serve this sweet and tart sauce with sweet potato fries or chicken tidbits for dipping.

- ◆ 1½ cups ketchup
- ◆ ½ cup honey mustard

In a small bowl, combine ketchup and honey mustard. Cover and serve as a dipping sauce.
Yield: 2 cups sauce

CREAMY CARAMEL FRUIT DIP

Dipping apple slices in a lemon juice and water mixture will keep them from turning dark.

- 1 package (8 ounces) cream cheese, softened
- ³/₄ cup firmly packed brown sugar
- 1 cup milk
- 1 package (3.4 ounces) vanilla instant pudding mix
- 2 teaspoons vanilla extract
- 2 teaspoons lemon juice
- 1 cup sour cream
- Red and green apple slices to serve

In a small bowl, beat cream cheese and brown sugar until smooth. Add milk, pudding mix, vanilla, and lemon juice; beat until smooth. Stir in sour cream. Cover and chill 2 hours. Serve with apple slices.
Yield: about 4 cups dip

CHRISTMAS PARTY SNACK MIX

Choose your child's favorite snacks to make this mix.

- 1 package (8 ounces) bite-size peanut butter sandwich cookies
- 1 package (6.6 ounces) fish-shaped Parmesan crackers
- 1 package (14 ounces) fruit-flavored jellybeans
- 1 package (6 ounces) chocolate-covered dried cranberries
- 1 package (5 ounces) yogurt-covered pretzels

Combine ingredients in a medium bowl. Store in an airtight container until ready to serve.
Yield: about 10 cups snack mix

SANTA STOP HERE ORNAMENT

Paint a plaque-style ornament (with attached hanger and bells) red and lightly sand to distress the edges. Use a paint pen to write "Santa Stop Here." Glue seasonal scrapbook paper to the ornament back. A cute paper flag (printed from your computer) tells Santa "I've been GOOD!!"

PEANUT BUTTER COOKIE POPS

Use a piece of rigid foam to stick dipped cookie pops in while drying.

◆ 16 peanut-shaped peanut butter sandwich cookies

◆ 4 ounces cream cheese, softened and cut into pieces

◆ 18 6" lollipop sticks

◆ 6 ounces vanilla candy coating

◆ ½ cup white chocolate chips

◆ Green and red nonpareils

In a medium food processor, process cookies until finely ground. Add cream cheese; process until blended. Shape mixture into 1" balls; place on a waxed paper-lined baking sheet. Chill 2 hours or until firm. Insert a lollipop stick into each ball.

In a double boiler, combine vanilla candy coating and white chocolate chips over hot, not simmering water; stir until smooth. Dip cookie balls in white chocolate mixture; sprinkle with nonpareils. Place cookie pops into rigid foam to set up.

Yield: 18 cookie pops

Cheerful touches

Add cheerful touches throughout your home with easy crafts
for the wall, table, or tree. These simple decorations also make
charming gifts for friends who share your love of the holidays.

Bed Spring Trees

FELT TREE

- bed spring (we got ours at a flea market)
- ⅓ yard of 36"w cream or green wool felt
- craft knife
- beads
- hot glue gun
- heavy-duty wire cutters

1. Cut the felt into 2" squares. Fold each square and cut a slit through all layers (*Fig. 1*).

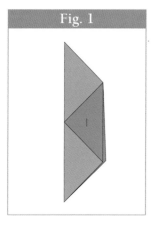

Fig. 1

2. Cut apart any joined area at the top of the bed spring. Slide the folded felt pieces on the spring, filling the entire spring.
3. Hot glue beads to the tree.

WIRED TREE

- bed spring (we got ours at a flea market)
- 18-gauge wire
- beads
- heavy-duty wire cutters

1. Cut a ring from the top of the bed spring; set aside.
2. Wrap the tree with the wire, beginning at the spring bottom and adding beads as desired.
3. Wrap the ring with wire and a bead. Attach the ring to the tree top with wire.

Framed Snowman

- 9" x 12" black picture frame
- 11" x 14" black and white fabric piece for background
- 10" x 13" tan fabric piece
- embroidery floss (white, red, and black)
- 4mm black beads for eyes
- orange felt scrap
- cream scrapbook paper
- fabric glue
- fusible tear-away embroidery stabilizer
- embroidery needle
- pinking shears
- tissue paper

Refer to Embroidery Stitches (page 57) and use 3 strands of floss for all embroidery.

1. Follow the manufacturer's instructions to fuse stabilizer to the wrong side of the tan fabric piece. Photocopy the pattern (page 64) at 118%. Trace onto tissue paper. Center and pin the tissue paper pattern on the right side of the tan fabric piece. Referring to the *Stitching Key* for stitches and floss colors, embroider the snowman. Sew on beads for the eyes. Cut an orange felt nose and glue to the face.

2. Use pinking shears to trim the embroidered piece to 6" x 9". Use black *Stem Stitches* to attach the embroidered piece to the background fabric. Print a holiday message on the cream scrapbook paper; tack above the snowman.

3. Wrap the background fabric around the frame backing and tape in place. Insert the backing in the frame.

"Celebrate" Banner

- nine 7" x 17" felt pieces
- 15" x 18" white felt piece
- nine fabric scraps for backgrounds
- 12" x 15" fabric piece for letters
- paper-backed fusible web
- 85" length of twill tape
- red embroidery floss
- 18 ³/₄" diameter buttons

1. Photocopy the patterns on page 60 at 193%. Freehand draw letters (about 3"-3³/₈" high) to spell "celebrate."
2. Use the frame pattern to cut 9 frames from the white felt. Matching the short ends, fold each remaining felt piece in half. Cut 9 pennants from felt, placing the pattern on the fold.
3. Fuse web to the wrong side of the fabrics. Use the drawn letter patterns to cut letters from letter fabric. Cut a 3" x 4¹/₈" piece from each background fabric.
4. Fuse the letters to the backgrounds. Fuse the backgrounds to the pennants. Use *Running Stitches* (page 57) to attach the frames to the pennants with 3 floss strands.
5. Placing the twill tape in the fold, arrange the pennants on the tape. Sew buttons to the pennant corners, stitching through all layers to secure the pennants to the twill tape.

"Good Cheer" Wall Hoop

- 10" diameter wooden embroidery hoop
- 14" square of white fabric for background
- fabric and felt scraps
- embroidery floss
- 1/2" diameter button
- embroidery needle
- acrylic paint and paintbrushes
- matte-finish clear acrylic spray sealer
- fabric glue
- fine-grit sandpaper

1. Paint the embroidery hoop rings. Once dry, lightly sand the edges. Working in a well-ventilated area, spray the rings with acrylic sealer.
2. Photocopy the pattern (page 61) at 125%. Tape the pattern to a sunny window; center and tape the background fabric over the pattern. Trace the pattern onto the background fabric. Use the pattern to cut 5 pennants, a wing, and a beak from fabric scraps. Cut the letters and body from felt scraps.
3. Machine stitch the bird and pennant pieces to the background fabric. Add the stitched "pennant hanger." Use 4 floss strands and *Stem Stitches* (page 57) to work "good" and 2 floss strands and *Running Stitches* to work the trail around the word and to outline the bird. Sew the button eye to the bird. Glue the felt letters to the pennants.
4. Center the stitched piece in the embroidery hoop and tighten the hoop; neatly trim away the excess fabric.

Paper Leaves Wreath

Photocopy the patterns (page 61) at 225%. Use the patterns to cut leaves from old Christmas song sheet music, brown paper, old books, old sewing pattern tissue, or scrapbook paper; use decorative-edged scissors to cut some of the leaves. Add a holiday message to some of leaves with rub-on letters.

Wrap a foam wreath with strips of pattern tissue. Pin the leaves to the wreath. Add a ribbon bow and some greenery to the top.

Knit Santa

 EASY +

Finished Size: about 12" tall

MATERIALS
Medium Weight Yarn
- Red - 40 yards
- Beige - 7 yards

Light Weight Yarn
- Black - 5 yards

Super Bulky Weight Novelty Yarn
- White - 30 yards

- Size 4 (3.5 mm) knitting needles
- Yarn needle
- Polyester fiberfill
- Wool roving for beard
- Felt scrap for eyes
- Scrapbook brad for belt buckle
- 6" length of ¹/₂" wide black satin ribbon for belt

Gauge is not of great importance; your Santa may be a little larger or smaller without changing the overall effect. The ornament is knit with a smaller size needle than normally used for the yarn weights in order to keep the fiberfill from showing through the stitches.

HEAD AND BODY
With Beige, cast on 18 sts, leaving an 18" end for sewing.

Row 1: Purl across.

Row 2 (Right side): Knit across.

Rows 3-12: Repeat Rows 1 and 2, 5 times.

Cut Beige.

Row 13 (Collar): With White, purl across.

Row 14: Knit across.

Cut White.
Row 15: With Red, purl across.
Row 16: Knit across.
Rows 17-36: Repeat Rows 15 and 16, 10 times.
Cut Red, leaving a long end for sewing.
Row 37: With White and leaving a long end for sewing, purl across.
Row 38: Knit across.
Row 39: Purl across.
Rows 40-43: Repeat Rows 38 and 39 twice.
Bind off all sts in **knit**.

EYES
Hold a felt scrap on inside of the Head and work 2 Black French Knots in center of Row 6, spaced 3 sts apart.

Weave the long end from the cast on edge through the cast on edge, gather tightly and secure the end. Use same end to sew back seam to Collar. Stuff Head lightly, then weave needle through sts on Row 13, gather tightly for neck and secure end.

With a 6" (15 cm) length of Red, weave needle through sts on Row 26 and gather moderately for waist. Using yarn ends, weave back seam. Flatten Body with seam centered at back. With a 6" (15 cm) length of White, sew bottom edge closed, stuffing Body lightly before closing.

ARM (Make 2)
With Black, cast on 8 sts leaving a 6" (15 cm) end for sewing.
Row 1: Purl across.
Row 2 (Right side): Knit across.
Rows 3 and 4: Repeat Rows 1 and 2. Cut Black.

Row 5: With White, purl across.
Row 6: Knit across.
Cut White.
Row 7: With Red, purl across.
Row 8: Knit across.
Rows 9-14: Repeat Rows 7 and 8, 3 times.
Cut yarn leaving a long end for sewing.
Thread yarn needle with long end and slip sts from knitting needle onto yarn, gather tightly and secure end. Use end to weave Arm back seam. Weave the long yarn end from the cast on edge through sts on cast on edge. Gather tightly and secure end.

Sew each Arm to Body below Collar.

LEG (Make 2)
With Black, cast on 10 sts leaving a 6" (15 cm) end for sewing.
Row 1: Purl across.
Row 2 (Right side): Knit across.
Rows 3-8: Repeat Rows 1 and 2, 3 times.
Cut Black, leaving a long end for sewing.
Row 9: With Red, purl across.
Row 10: Knit across.
Rows 11-17: Repeat Rows 9 and 10, 3 times; then repeat Row 9 once **more**.
Cut yarn, leaving a long end for sewing.
Thread yarn needle with long end and slip sts from knitting needle onto yarn, gather tightly and secure end. Use yarn ends to weave Leg back seam. Lightly stuff Leg. Flatten Leg with seam centered at back. With a 6" (15 cm) length of Black, sew bottom edge closed.

Sew each Leg to Body.

HAT
With White, cast on 3 sts.
Row 1: Purl across.
Row 2 (Right side): Knit across.
Rows 3 and 4: Repeat Rows 1 and 2. Cut White.
Row 5: With Red, purl across.
Row 6: Knit across.
Row 7: Purl across.
Row 8: Increase (knit into front of next stitch, knit into back of same stitch), knit 1, increase: 5 sts.
Row 9: Purl across.
Row 10 (Increase row): Increase, knit across to last st, increase: 7 sts.
Rows 11-30: Repeat Rows 9 and 10, 10 times: 27 sts.
Cut Red, leaving a long end for sewing.
Row 31: With White, purl across.
Row 32: Knit across.
Rows 33-37: Repeat Rows 31 and 32 twice, then repeat Row 31 once **more**.
Bind off all sts in **knit**, leaving a long end for sewing.

Using yarn ends, weave back seam. Put Hat on Head, pulling back edge of Hat close to Collar edge. With long end from bind off edge, sew Hat to Head.

FINISHING
Pull small sections [about 4" long] of roving apart. Arrange on Head, covering the whole Head; sew to head across the center. Fold the top portion of roving down; shape and trim beard as desired.
Wrap ribbon around waist, overlap ends, and insert brad.
Add a Red hanging loop to the Hat front.

General Instructions

SIZING PHOTOS

To change the size of a photo, divide the desired height or width of the photo (whichever is larger) by the actual height or width of the photo. Multiply the result by 100 and photocopy the photo at this percentage.

For example: You want your photo to be 8" high, but the actual photo is 6" high.

So 8 DIVIDED BY 6 = 1.33 x 100 = 133%. Copy the photo at 133%.

MAKING POM-POMS

Cut a piece of cardboard 3" wide and as long as you want the diameter of your finished pom-pom to be. Wind the yarn around the cardboard – the more you wrap, the fluffier the pom-pom (*Fig. 1*).

Carefully slip the yarn off the cardboard and firmly tie an 18" length of yarn around the middle (*Fig. 2*). Leave yarn ends long enough to attach the pom-pom. Cut the loops on both ends and trim the pom-pom into a smooth ball (*Fig. 3*).

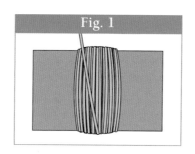
Fig. 1

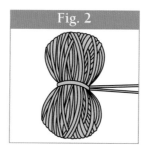
Fig. 2

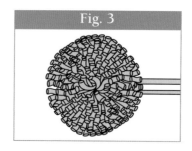
Fig. 3

DYEING POM-POMS

Dyeing pom-poms is quite easy. We used several shades of red, burgundy, and orange dye, mixing the shades to increase the color palette. Try using white, pink, red, yellow, and brown pom-poms for a variety of berry colors. Since the pom-poms are not rinsed after dyeing, they are not color-fast.

Add 4 teaspoons of powdered fabric dye to 4 cups very hot water in a disposable plastic container; stir until the dye is dissolved. Add the pom-poms, squeeze the dye into the pom-poms, and let soak at least 5 minutes. For darker colors, leave the pom-poms in the dye longer.

Remove the pom-poms from the dye and let dry undisturbed for 2 days on a paper towel-lined baking sheet.

EMBROIDERY STITCHES

Follow the Stitch Diagrams to bring the needle up at odd numbers and down at even numbers.

Backstitch

Chain Stitch

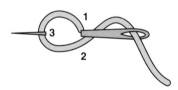

Couch Stitch

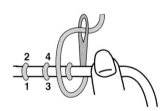

French Knot

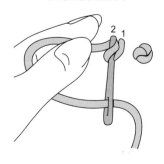

Running Stitch

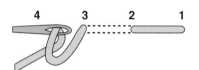

Satin Stitch

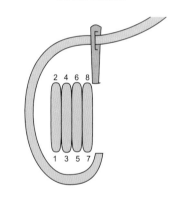

Stem Stitch

Straight Stitch

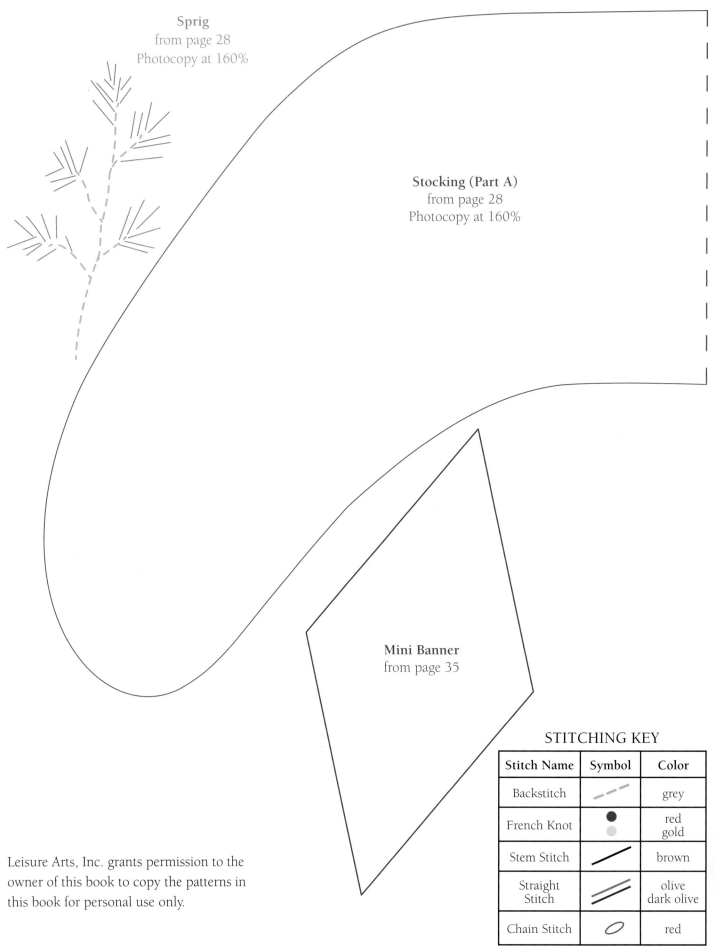

Sprig
from page 28
Photocopy at 160%

Stocking (Part A)
from page 28
Photocopy at 160%

Mini Banner
from page 35

Leisure Arts, Inc. grants permission to the
owner of this book to copy the patterns in
this book for personal use only.

STITCHING KEY

Stitch Name	Symbol	Color
Backstitch		grey
French Knot	● ●	red gold
Stem Stitch		brown
Straight Stitch		olive dark olive
Chain Stitch	⬭	red

Stocking (Part B)
from page 28
Photocopy at 160%

"Joy" Banner
from page 18

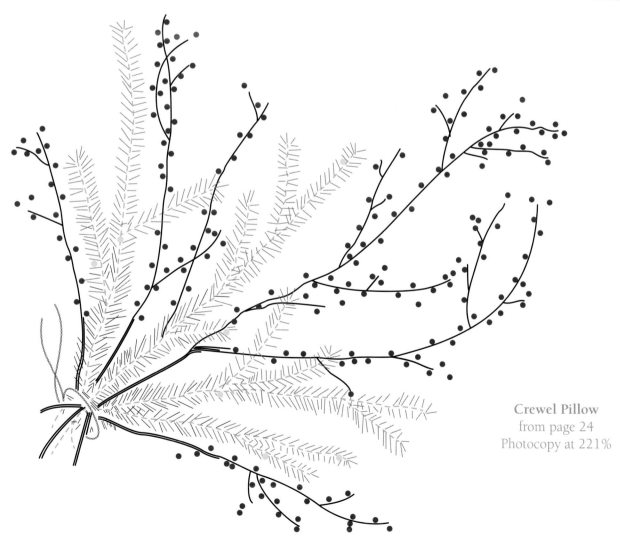

Crewel Pillow
from page 24
Photocopy at 221%

"Celebrate" Banner
from page 52
Photocopy at 193%

Elf Hat
from page 17
Photocopy at 255% for heads up to 21" diameter
Photocopy at 277% for heads over 21" diameter

"Good" Cheer Wall Hoop
from page 53
Photocopy at 125%

Pom-Pom Flowers
from page 20
Photocopy at 118%

Leaf Wreath
from page 53
Photocopy at 225%

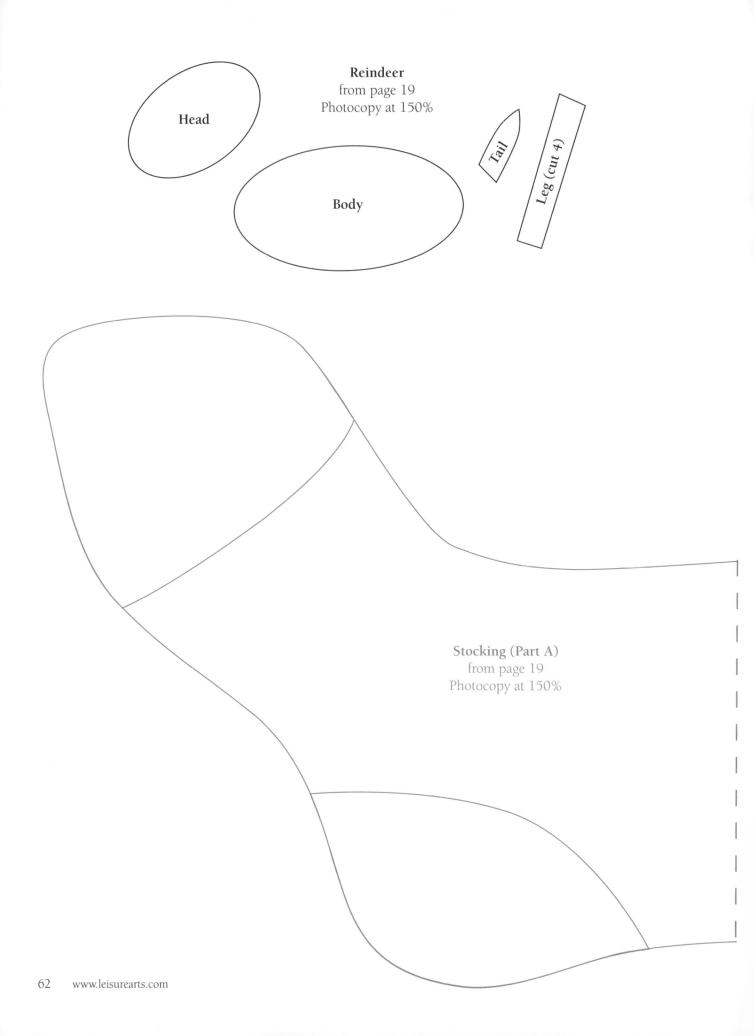

Reindeer
from page 19
Photocopy at 150%

Head

Body

Tail

Leg (cut 4)

Stocking (Part A)
from page 19
Photocopy at 150%

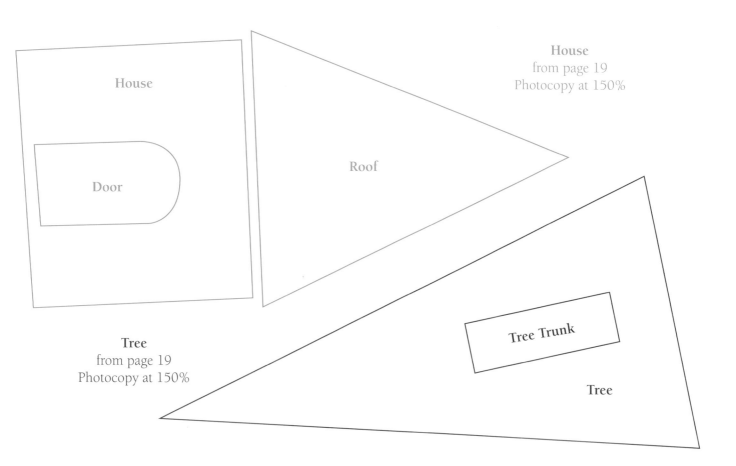

House

House

Door

House
from page 19
Photocopy at 150%

Roof

Tree
from page 19
Photocopy at 150%

Tree Trunk

Tree

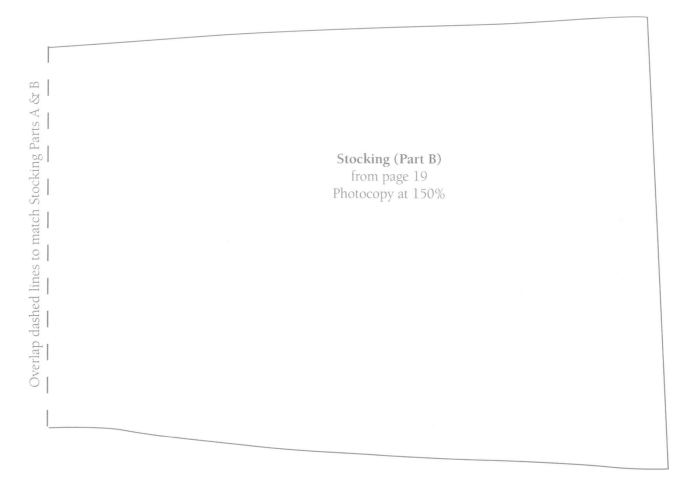

Overlap dashed lines to match Stocking Parts A & B

Stocking (Part B)
from page 19
Photocopy at 150%

Framed Snowman
from page 51
Photocopy at 118%

STITCHING KEY

Stitch Name	Symbol	Color
Backstitch		black
French Knot		red white
Stem Stitch		red white black
Straight Stitch		white
Satin Stitch		red white black

Fill in with white Stem Stitches worked in a continuous spiral.

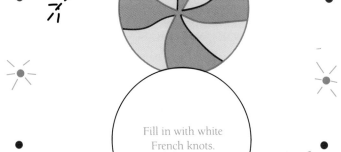

Fill in with white French knots.

Banner
from page 35
Burlap Shapes - Photocopy at 197%
Cardstock Shapes - Photocopy at 189%

Pennant Garland
from page 15